What is Language Deprivation?

D1716305

Avril Hertneky

ISBN: 9798431970962

Editing by Jennifer Avril Hertneky.
www.fromrejectiontolove.com

Layout by Arash Jahani
Cover Design by Arash Jahani

WHAT IS LANGUAGE DEPRIVATION?

Written by: Avril Hertneky

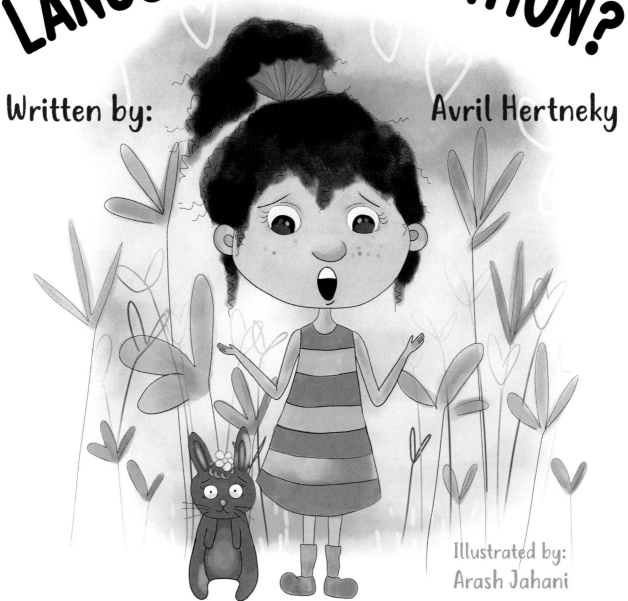

Illustrated by:
Arash Jahani

This is based on a true story.

To all Deaf Children, I hope you enjoy
this book and that you find the courage
to overcome any fears you may have,
like I did.

Love from Avril Hertneky.

I am Avril.
I am Deaf.
I cannot hear
any sounds!

Avril can only feel vibrations!

Everybody knows I am Deaf.

My parents and siblings refused to learn
sign language to communicate with me.

Avril feels sad
and lonely.

I do not know how old I am. I do not know what my name is.

I do not understand
the subjects at the public school I went to.

Everybody was talking, eating, and laughing. They did not share what they were saying with me.

I was forced to communicate with spoken language.

My television never had the Closed Caption turned on.

I have always struggled with how to communicate and how to express myself.

I was not allowed to go to the sleepovers.

I never have
bedtime stories.

I walked into the classroom at the Deaf school.

I saw the kids signing.

Watching them sign are so beautiful!

I learned to write my name.

I am 8 years old.
I now know
how old I am.

I learned
all the subjects!

My friends and I are using sign language.
We laughed together.

I felt so loved.

A Deaf teacher is telling us a story!

I am so happy about
my dream.

Use the statements and questions below to start having a conversation about language deprivation:

What is the communication barrier?

Who can you talk to about your fear or struggle at home and how to overcome it?

Once you have faced your language barrier and overcome it, how do you think you will feel?

What was a situation where you felt scared and are now brave?

No one should have to go through what I went through. If you know of someone who is going through these types of experiences, ask them to have professional help and get the state/ provinces involved for one's protection and those of children.

3 out of 1,000 Children are Deaf or Hard of Harding have Language Deprivation. Start learn Sign Language now, not later.

#SaveDeafChildren

If you want to learn more about Avril Hertneky and her new books, go to

Website: www.fromrejectiontolove.com
Email: fromrejectiontolove@gmail.com

Made in the USA
Monee, IL
14 December 2022

21485535R00024